Eat, Drink, and Be Merry
Lessons from Ecclesiastes

By Lucas Doremus

First published 2020

Copyright © 2020 by Lucas Doremus

All rights reserved. No part of this publication may be reproduced, stored, or transmitted in any form or by any means, electronic, mechanical, photocopying, recording, scanning, or otherwise without written permission from the publisher. It is illegal to copy this book, post it to a website, or distribute it by any other means without permission.

All Scripture quotations taken from the New King James Version unless otherwise indicated.

Cover photo: "King Solomon," Simeon Solomon, Public domain, via Wikimedia Commons

Cover design by Sarah Doremus

First edition

Contents

Overview of Ecclesiastes

Chapter 1..1
  Introduction
    1:1-1:11

Chapter 2..4
  Solomon's Goal, Achievements, and a Conclusion
    1:12-2:26

Chapter 3..13
  A Time for Everything
    3:1-3:8

Chapter 4..16
  The Second Conclusion
    3:9-3:15

Chapter 5..19
  Moreover, Then, Again, Then
    3:16-4:16

Chapter 6..24
  First Commands
    5:1-5:8

Chapter 7..27
  Money and Possessions
    5:9-5:20

Chapter 8..31
  Labor
    6:1-6:12

Chapter 9..34
  Comparisons and Wisdom
    7:1-7:14

Chapter 10..40
  More Observations and a Conclusion
    7:15-8:1
Chapter 11..48
  The King and Us
    8:2-8:9
Chapter 12..51
  The Reality of Death
    8:10-:9:10
Chapter 13..56
  The Return
    9:11-10:20
Chapter 14..63
  Observations About Work
    11:1-11:8
Chapter 15..66
  To the Young Man
    11:9-12:8
Chapter 16..68
  Solomon's Afterword
    12:9-12:14

To Sarah, Elijah, and Dexter,
Thank you for making my heritage so full of joy.

I can imagine sitting across from an aged Solomon listening to the wisdom of the most sagacious man that ever lived. Speaking with a soft voice, he tells me what he has learned over his achievement filled life, but he can't help but give me very practical advice in between his stories. Never in a commanding "Do this or else" way but as an experienced elder who wants a young man to avoid the mistakes he made in his life. I would be listening as closely as I can, not wanting to miss a word. After leaving his presence, everything he said would be a blur as I try to put it all together in a way I can apply it to my life and impart his wisdom to those I know.

As I read through Ecclesiastes, this scenario is how I imagine what was written down: Solomon documenting what he learned in life with helpful proverbs along the way. It can be difficult to conceive why God wanted this type of book in His canon. It is different from any other book and can sometimes seem contradictory to the companion book, Proverbs.

It is easy to lose sight of what God is trying to teach us in this great book. I have spent a lot of time in Ecclesiastes trying to absorb the wisdom at a young age what can only be experienced after a long life. I believe this book is relevant at any age but requires a very honest look at what life is and what life isn't. The most important theme throughout Ecclesiastes is to trust God through toil on this Earth. We will see this theme frequently mentioned by

Solomon.

If you can view life through the lens of faith, you will have life abounding in joy. That is the purpose of this commentary: to give an understanding of the book of Ecclesiastes and point to faith in God as the only way to understand and enjoy life on this Earth.

Overview of Ecclesiastes

One of the most difficult aspects of understanding Ecclesiastes is the structure of the book. At first glance it seems very unorganized. However, getting to know how Solomon writes is key to grasping the flow of the book. Song of Solomon is not as helpful to understanding this writing, as the style is very different from Ecclesiastes. Proverbs on the other hand, gives us great insight on how Solomon structures more focused wisdom literature.

The first nine chapters of Proverbs feature longer discourses on different subjects, centering around wisdom. The constant repetition of "My son" in these chapters shows the compassionate teacher in Solomon. We can see this in Ecclesiastes as well in 12:9-10. By contrast, chapters 10-29 in Proverbs feature mostly short proverbs of differing types, such as parallel and contrasting statements, commands, comparisons, and thought-provoking questions.

In Ecclesiastes, we see the same style but with discourses on Solomon's personal life; there are only 27 commands in the book, as opposed to Proverbs, which has many more. Solomon will talk awhile about his experiences, conclude them with a lesson, tell a few proverbs, and then go back into his life story, which is often how an older person might teach. The personal sections are recognized by the pronoun "I," while the proverbial sections sound like something you would read in Proverbs and are more general to life.

utlining the book in Solomon's shifts between personal experiences and proverbial sections helps to understand the flow of thought. The exact break between sections are not always clear, as Solomon may state he has seen something and proceed to tell a few general proverbs not necessarily related to his life. I have used this general pattern to outline Ecclesiastes and the chapters of this commentary. An added layer of difficulty arises from the chapter and verse divisions, which are in my opinion not helpful and even distracting when reading through the book.

Understanding the main theme of Ecclesiastes is as important as the structure. The thesis throughout Ecclesiastes is faith in God- all of the evils, vanities, and observations are always pointing back to God as the origin of everything, underscoring how we should trust Him with everything. Interestingly, the word "faith" never appears in Ecclesiastes, although the Old Testament concept of fear does. Faith is obviously one of the main themes throughout the Bible, and Ecclesiastes is no exception.

Another important aspect of understanding Ecclesiastes is repeated words and questions types. One such repeated word is "vanity," repeated 36 times throughout the book. The phrase "my heart" is repeated 18 times. When you put these two together, you get one of the central points of the book: living for "my heart" is nothing but "vanity."

There are 28 questions that Solomon asks throughout the book: there are two "hows," five "whys", ten "whats," and eleven "whos". These questions vary in the subject matter, but this tally made me see that Ecclesiastes is more about Who, than about what, why, or how. This is made even more clear from Solomon's conclusions throughout the book (2:24, 3:22, 5:18, 8:15, 9:7, 12:13).

As a final point in understanding Ecclesiastes, this commentary is simply a man-made attempt at understanding Solomon's last biblical writing. 12:12 says "Of making many books there is no end." I hope this book helps you to understand the book of Ecclesiastes, but there will always be more value in reading and studying the Bible than holding onto this imperfect commentary.

With all of that said, the best course of action is to put down this book and read Ecclesiastes many times over a few days. Try not to spend too much time doing intense study; read it straight through to get the flow of thought. After you begin to understand the overall structure and lessons, then go back and study more deeply. After you've done all that, continue reading this book. The more familiar you are with Ecclesiastes the more you will benefit from this book. See you when you finish!

Chapter 1

Introduction
1:1-11

In the first discourse of Ecclesiastes, Solomon gives us an overview of what he has seen in life.

1:1-11

The first verse tells us the book is written by the Preacher. Solomon is nowhere mentioned as the author of the book, but internal evidence can only point to him as the author. The Hebrew word translated "Preacher" means just that, as well as "collector" and "public speaker". Solomon refers to himself this way because of what life has taught him and that's what he is/does, as he says in 12:9.

The opening poetic statement repeats "vanity" 5 times. No need to ask Solomon, "Tell me what you really think about life." The next verse qualifies what he is talking about: profit from labor. The answer to this question is given through four examples of things on the Earth that have no outcome but are a continual cycle producing nothing different from cycle to cycle (v. 4-7):

1. The Earth persists while people die
2. The sun's path is the same every day
3. The winds follow the same basic circuit
4. The water cycle continually flows

The implied answer to the question in verse 3 is no- there is no profit from labor. The four examples then explain in a poetic way why this is so.

Verse 8 is a summary of these four examples of vanity. Man must toil and deal with each of these things, but his work is not satisfying because there is nothing to show from the labor. Verses 9-11 are a more detailed explanation of vanity that Solomon has been describing. Man has been dealing with vanity since "ancient times" and will continue to toil under the sun.

Subsequent generations will not remember the work that was completed by former generations and this continues for all history. Yes, we can see what was built and labored for, but we don't remember the people that were involved. We may know their name and a few facts about them, but we have no memories of their life.

These realizations bring us one of the first problems when trying to study the implications of Ecclesiastes. We as New Testament Church Age believers know that God tells us to work for Him and He will give us rewards in Heaven for our work. So how can Solomon say there is no profit when the illumination of the New Testament proves there is?

Eat, Drink, and Be Merry

The answer to this is in the context of what Solomon is talking about. Solomon is not speaking about eternal rewards or salvation at any point in his book. He is always talking about temporal work and temporal profit from that work. It is easy to read eternal meanings into certain passages, but that is not the way this book is to be understood. Whatever accomplishments you achieve on Earth cease when you die. That is the reality that Solomon addresses in chapter 3. All the problems you have also die when you die. Sort of sad, sort of comforting, isn't it?

Ecclesiastes must be interpreted through this earthly-life lens as well as Old Testament historical context. God did not reveal as much truth about the afterlife to Old Testament believers as He would reveal later in the New Testament; we cannot read these revelations back into Ecclesiastes when interpreting a passage. If we do that, we are necessarily saying Solomon could not understand what God was revealing to him to write. We must seek to understand this book as Solomon intended it, which means the entire book must be understood as talking about earthly life as outlined in the first eleven verses.

Chapter 2

Solomon's Goal, Achievements, and a Conclusion
1:12 - 2:26

In 1:12-18 Solomon gives us some background as to why he is writing Ecclesiastes. I view the first eleven verses of the book as being his conclusion (even though it appears at the beginning), then in this section he tells us the thoughts that launched him on the journey that led to this conclusion.

1:12-18

Solomon makes a reference to himself being the Preacher as well as king over Jerusalem. These two positions may tell us how Solomon wanted to be perceived by the people of Israel. If you live in a governmental system with a king, you will listen to him because of his position and the power he wields over you. Solomon being the Preacher and the king shows what kind of king he was. 12:9-10 tells us that Solomon taught the people and was always seeking truth in what was being taught. Solomon was flawed but cared much for the people of his kingdom.

Verse 13 and 14 give us what we would call the

"purpose statement" of Ecclesiastes. Solomon is trying to understand why we work on Earth. Here we have the first reference to the origin of this work: God. God has given work to men. Why? So we may be exercised by it. Work was given to Adam in the Garden of Eden before the fall, so there is nothing sinful about work (Gen 2:15). When God gave work to Adam before the Fall to take care of the creation it was not toilsome but enjoyable.

Since the Fall, work has taken on a different character. The word translated "exercised" in this verse carries the imagery of affliction. Jeremiah 17:10 says "I, the LORD, search the heart, I test the mind, even to give every man according to his ways, according to the fruit of his doings." God uses the toilsome work, which we have brought on ourselves because of our sin, to exercise us. There are more ways God uses the work He gives us, which Solomon will tell us as Ecclesiastes unfolds.

Of all the work we receive, none of it profits us temporally, as verse 14 explains. The next verse is the first insertion of a proverb from Solomon. Since God has given us the work, it cannot be made straight if it is crooked. If it is lacking in quantity, it cannot be numbered or counted above zero. To put it in modern vernacular, "you get what God gives you."

After deciding to search out the work done on Earth, Solomon assesses his ability to do so. He knows he has great wisdom because God gave it to him. But then he realizes that knowing wisdom and folly is grasping for the wind. Why? Because there are some things that we just cannot know. We can know what God revealed, but He has kept some things from us (Deuteronomy 29:29). We will go further into detail on this matter in chapter 10.

Solomon also says, "a man cannot find out the work that is done under the sun" (8:17). That is why we must walk by faith (2 Cor 5:7). God has set up the world and the work He gives us so that we will trust Him. The investigation into discovering the "why" behind it all is grasping for the wind because God won't allow you to find it, for then you would not need to trust Him. Solomon then concludes that this pursuit produces grief and sorrow. It is better to trust the perfect One who gives you work then to chase the winds of why.

2:1-10

Solomon starts his pursuit by testing his heart with three things: joy, wine, and great projects and works. The test of joy or mirth seems to have ended quickly; in the same verse Solomon tells us he is testing with joy, he says it is vanity. The next verse he says laughter is madness or foolishness and realizes mirth doesn't accomplish anything. Some secular philosophies (such as utilitarianism) have held that happiness or absence of unhappiness is the only thing sought for itself. Therefore, happiness is the ultimate goal of life. These philosophies may not use the word

Eat, Drink, and Be Merry

happiness, but rather a lack of suffering, which amounts to the same ideal. Solomon tells us this quest accomplishes nothing and is foolishness.

Solomon next tests his heart with wine. He tells us he is not getting drunk and he is not doing stupid things while he drinks. Apparently, this trial period didn't last long either, as he moves directly into his next test of projects and work. Wine clearly did not satisfy or answer anything that Solomon was trying to discover.

Verses 4-8 explain the wealth and projects that Solomon completed. The list is general here, but more detail is given in 1 Kings 4-10. Solomon had it all. There has been no one greater in Jerusalem, or arguably in history, that had more than Solomon. Knowing this, it should speak loudly to us that he has already said and will explain in detail that all of this is worth nothing.

The reward he received from the labor was the joy he got from doing the labor as verse 10 explains. This is the first mention of something positive in Ecclesiastes, but it is soon eclipsed by the rest of chapter 2. The word "then" is written five times as Solomon realizes five truths from his three tests. He then concludes the whole matter with the first "nothing is better" statement in verse 24.

2:11

Solomon's first assessment of his achievements is

the realization that there was no profit to all these works. It is vanity and grasping for the wind. Why? Because there is no profit which will last beyond the grave. The grave is a main theme throughout Ecclesiastes to demonstrate why all the work under the sun is vanity.

2:12

Directly relating to 1:17, Solomon considers wisdom, madness, and folly. He moved on from looking at his works because if his works are vanity, no one is going to build greater than he- they can only copy his achievements.

2:13-14

Solomon realizes that wisdom is better than foolishness. Here is another great problem when trying to interpret Ecclesiastes. If everything is vanity, why does anything I do whether wise or foolish matter?

Just because our works here on Earth are worthless in a temporal sense doesn't negate anything else said about doing works in Scripture. Proverbs, for instance, is full of practical ways to live your life. Ecclesiastes gives a context to how you are to view why you are doing what God has given you to do. God said it's better to be wise than to be foolish but being wise for your own sake and work yields vanity (1:17-18).

In verse 14, Solomon explains that wise men know what they are doing (eyes in his head), and a fool doesn't know what he is doing (walks in darkness). Yet, he says, the same event happens to them all. This event is death, which Solomon toils with for the rest of this section. Why should we bother being wise if we all die?

2:15-17

It is vanity to be wise if that wisdom only produces works here on Earth. You won't be remembered for who you are, so there is no profit. The natural outcome of this reasoning is to hate your life, which is exactly what Solomon falls into. The word translated "distressing" carries the meaning of being miserable. I believe Solomon may have gone into a depression because he realized none of his wisdom aimed at accomplishments produced anything that will last beyond his death for him to enjoy.

2:18-23

The last "then" explains Solomon's conclusions to his four revelations. His first realization is that someone else will inherit everything he has done. Solomon doesn't know if that person will handle it wisely or foolishly, which he comments is vanity.

When we die, we ultimately don't know how the people after us will treat what we have built. Even if they have good intentions, circumstances could drastically change, and they might not be able to take care of what we left. This is vanity, as Solomon says.

Solomon's depression gets deeper as the word "despaired" is used in verse 20; the Hebrew word used in this instance carries the imagery of being without hope. Job experienced this same lack of hope which is why he questioned God (Job 6:11, 7:6, 14:14, 30:26). Job could not see his situation changing from his suffering, which is what caused the lack of hope. Solomon is seeing the same thing, that nothing he can do will change the vanity of his accomplishments.

Solomon further comments that this situation of hopelessness is a great evil. Verse 22 could be an effort to break the depression as Solomon asks if there is anything to be gained from all the toil under the sun, trying to find something of value in his work. His days have been sorrowful and hard; what is it worth? Furthermore, a night's rest is not restful because a man must repeat the same labor tomorrow.

2:24-26

This is the first of four "nothing is better" statements in Ecclesiastes. Each time we get more information centered around the theme of Who the work is from and what we should do about it. Understanding these four conclusions as well as the other two like them tells us exactly the lessons that God wants us to learn from this great book.

First of all, we should eat, drink, and enjoy good in our labor. Since there is no lasting profit from our labor, the experience of the labor itself is to be valued (2:10). All of this, as Solomon says, is from the hand or power of God.

You are able to eat, drink, and work because God gave those abilities to you. He also gave you the physical elements that you eat and drink. The most important part of this conclusion is Who all these things come from. If none of our works last, and we cannot do anything that Solomon didn't do (2:25), then enjoying what God gives us in the moment is the sum total of how to conduct ourselves while here on Earth.

If we enjoy these things, God gives us wisdom, knowledge, and joy. This follows the general principle that God always has for His people throughout time: if you live how God instructs you, things generally go well. If you live opposite to how God instructs you, things generally go badly. If God says He gives wisdom, knowledge, and joy to those following Him, whose fault is it when we are without these things? Ours! When God makes promises to give us things and we don't receive them, it is always our fault. James makes this clear when he says:

> But let him ask in faith, with no doubting, for he who doubts is like a wave of the sea driven and

tossed by the wind. For let not that man suppose that he will receive anything from the Lord.
James 1:6-7

For those who live against God's commands, Solomon says God gives him the job of gathering and collecting to give the product to the good. Since they are not looking to God for fulfillment in their labor, they have nothing to work for but to keep themselves and the good alive. But in the end, it is all vanity and grasping for the wind because after they all die, there is nothing they can take with them.

Chapter 3

A Time for Everything
3:1-8

The first proverbial section might be addressing a logical thought in the reader's mind after finishing chapter 2: if I'm supposed to enjoy all my work, what about all the bad parts of life I must go through? It could also be a continuation of the thought chapter 2 ended with, namely that gathering and collecting is the job of the sinner. Either way, the conclusion is that all work is from the hand of God, even the circumstances of different seasons of life.

3:1-8

Verse 1 says "for every purpose" under heaven. We already know that one reason God gives us labor is to exercise us (1:13). These eight verses make it clear that the good parts of our life and the bad are both from God.

It is important at this juncture to make the point of sticking to what the text says when interpreting the Bible and not what we think it implies, especially when reading Ecclesiastes. There is no instruction given on what to do with any of the contrasts in these eight verses. For instance, there is a time to laugh and a time to mourn. Nowhere in the text of this section is it saying when to laugh or mourn. We can make some obvious guesses on when to do one or the other, but without doing a study in the Bible on the two contrasting subjects or timing of life's circumstances, we would be putting our own meaning on the text instead of letting the text speak for itself.

Isaiah gives us a parable on how God views timing of life's happenings:

> Give ear and hear my voice,
> Listen and hear my speech.
> Does the plowman keep plowing all day to sow?
> Does he keep turning his soil and breaking the clods?
> When he has leveled its surface,
> Does he not sow the black cummin
> And scatter the cummin,
> Plant the wheat in rows,
> The barley in the appointed place,
> And the spelt in its place?
> For He instructs him in right judgement,
> His God teaches him.
> For the black cummin is not threshed with a threshing sledge,
> Nor is a cartwheel rolled over the cummin;
> But the black cummin is beaten out with a stick,
> And the cummin with a rod.
> Bread flour must be ground;

> Therefore he does not thresh it forever,
> Break it with his cartwheel,
> Or crush it with his horsemen.
> This also comes from the LORD of hosts,
> Who is wonderful in counsel and excellent in guidance.
> *Isaiah 28:23-29*

The context of this passage is God talking to the nation of Israel about how His timing of prophetic events is much like a farmer's timing of work. A farmer knows when to do or stop different tasks. Notice also that God is the one who teaches him these things. The farmer also knows how to treat different crops in the correct way. The passage concludes with a statement that these things are from the LORD of Hosts (2nd person of the Trinity) just like Ecclesiastes says our work is from God (2:24). The lesson learned is that we should trust God's timing for world events. And if we can trust Him for big events, we can trust Him for our lives as well.

To conclude this section of scripture, Solomon only asks the reader to realize there is a time for everything, making no state of anything relating to our lives perpetual even when we are without hope. Since we can make the connection that these timings are all from God, we should not try to figure out exactly when all these contrasts should occur or why they occur, but trust God that His timings are righteous.

Chapter 4

The Second Conclusion
3:9-15

Since our lives and what is done in them is not static, Solomon again asks the question "what profit is gained?"

3:9-11

The first time this question was asked appeared in 1:3 where it was a very general question to all of life. Now it is more specific because of the mention in verse 11 that everything has been made beautiful in its time by God. The same verse also says that we have eternity in our hearts; this means we are looking for things to last into eternity. Most of us don't like change and would like certain items to last forever- a pair of shoes, a car, or furniture. But things deteriorate and we must replace old things with new. Or, for instance, our car is hit by someone, making the replacement necessary immediately. Why is this so? Solomon says you are not able to find out the work of God which God gives in verse 11.

In verse 10 we are given the second reason that God gives us work: we are to be occupied with it.

When God put Adam in the Garden, He gave him work. I believe that God will have plenty of work for us to do when we are in Heaven. No longer will we be exercised by it in the sense we are now, but it will be perfect work that we not only enjoy but will never tire of doing. Revelation 22:3 says that we shall serve God in the Eternal State, by implication through our work. What a wonderful thing to be occupied with for eternity!

3:12-15

The next "nothing is better" statement tells us to rejoice and do good in addition to eating, drinking, and enjoying good in labor. Another very important detail is included, that these things are a gift of God just as salvation is a gift of God received by faith in Jesus Christ dying for our sins on the cross. Salvation is only effective to those who receive the gift by faith; the joy we receive from our labor is only effective when we receive it by faith.

Without faith, work is not typically viewed as something to rejoice in. Whether a man is "living for the weekend" or working only to receive a paycheck to spend on his hobbies, work is not viewed as a gift in which he should rejoice. Here we start to see that Ecclesiastes is more about "Who" than what or why, as stated in the overview of this commentary.

Moving on to more information about why we should rejoice in our labor, verse 14 basically says

"God does what He wants." Why does God do what He does? So men should fear Him. The Hebrew word translated "fear" carries the meaning of plain fear, but also reverence, a respect that should border on fear. We are told to fear God (Matt 10:28, Luke 12:5), so I am careful here not to exclude that fact. But the reverence aspect of this word includes our great veneration for who God is.

To bring these verses together including the beginning of chapter 3, when God gives us work, He knows the time and purpose for it. He also affords us the ability to rejoice in it which means we should always trust Him with whatever He gives us. As verse 15 says, God will not give us anything that He has not given to mankind in the past (nothing new under the sun), and He will require an account of what we did with what He gave us. Reader, will you choose to rejoice because you having nothing better to do with what you have been given? Or will you grasp for the wind?

Chapter 5

Moreover, Then, Again, Then
3:16 - 4:16

There are four observations that Solomon makes in the next section. I believe he is continuing the section that took a brief pause at the end of chapter 2 to continue his journey in understanding all that is done under Heaven (1:13). He also begins using the phrase "my heart" again to bring us back to his initial purpose. Until this point, Solomon has only looked at his life and what it hasn't produced. He begins expanding the scope of his expedition by looking at the world around him.

3:16-22

Solomon introduces the first observation with the word "moreover." He notices the inequalities of life after making some conclusions on his initial reflections (2:24, 3:12). On Earth, sometimes justice is not done and wickedness prevails. In the end, Solomon knows that God will judge every work done under Heaven. However, it is according to His timing and purpose, which should bring to our remembrance 3:1-8.

3:16 - 4:16

Solomon communes with his heart and gives us another reason God gives us work, or the condition of the sons of men: to test us. Why does He test us? So that we see we are like animals and will die. Mankind is the pinnacle of creation (Genesis 1:26), but in the sense of being mortal, we are no different than any other living thing. Verse 21 explains part of this distinction by telling us that the spirit of a man goes upward and the spirit of an animal goes downward. This means that our soul lives forever in the eternal places, either Heaven or Hell, and the soul of an animal goes to the Earth, thus not living forever.

Because of our mortality and the inequalities of life, Solomon concludes that man should rejoice in our third "nothing is better" statement. Another detail is then included; it is our heritage to rejoice in the work God gave us. The Hebrew word in this context means "to divide out in a share or apportion." What could be more special than an individualized portion of God's plan created directly from the Creator of the universe just for you? And you should enjoy your part, because you do not know what will happen after you are gone, as Solomon states in the same verse.

4:1-3

The next thing Solomon notices is the oppression on Earth. He divides people into two categories: the oppressed and the oppressors. Neither have a comforter, which is the problem Solomon sees. When you are oppressed you should have a comforter to help you to deal with the oppression, but apparently those in power need comforters, too. I believe this is because power brings sorrow just as wisdom brings sorrow (1:18), and Solomon, being king, knew this well. In both cases of being oppressed and oppressing, comfort is needed.

Because of this fact, Solomon praises those who have never been born, who do not have to deal with the evil done under the sun. This is a strange fact as we immediately think "but if we believe in Christ and go to Heaven, of course it's better to be born!" Ecclesiastes is only talking about temporal things, so in the context with which Solomon is dealing, it is better to not deal with all this evil on Earth than having to live with it. Jesus also says of Judas "It would have been good for that man if he had never been born!" (Matthew 26:24, Mark 14:21). There must be a sense in which never existing is better than the toil we encounter on Earth or the consequences of our choices. This concept is explored further in chapter 6 when Solomon visits this idea again with different circumstances.

4:4-6

The third observation is how we envy each other for our accomplishments and skills. Solomon immediately comments that this is vanity and grasping for the wind. The Bible is very clear that we are not to be jealous of others, and this passage provides a great example of this since we were just told that God has planned a heritage just for us. Furthermore, God is the one who gave us our individualized talents. If we wish for different skills, we are, in a way, rejecting what God gave us. How strange to think the coveting is more than selfishness but a rejection of our heritage from God.

Verse 15 indicates that the one who is jealous is also lazy and a fool. The phrase "folds his hands" means to be lazy and "consumes his own flesh" means to waste what he has. I believe the implication of this is that jealousy is connected to not working hard. When a man is jealous, he is not only diminishing what skills he has but putting his energy toward desire instead of work. The proverb that follows means it is better to realize what you have without jealousy (even if it is small) than the baggage and work that comes with envy that does not profit anything.

4:7-16

The final observation is split into three sections that deal with companionship- or more accurately, the lack thereof. Each of the three are called vanity in verse 7, but the first and the third are mentioned as being vanity specifically. In terms of their subject matter, these two seem worse than the second.

The first observation speaks of someone who has no companion; no family, no wife, nor children. Yet he must work the same as everyone else, and he is never satisfied with money. The implied answer of his question ("For whom do I toil and deprive myself of good") is no one. He doesn't work or deprive himself of good for anyone. He has only himself, which is not satisfying. Solomon comments this is a grave misfortune.

He continues after this small conclusion that two are better than one. Why? Because they can help each other when one falls. This is why the reward for their labor is good. A man without a companion to help him has a woe placed upon him. When there are two companions, they can keep each other warm and defend each other when an oppressor is tyrannizing them. In this case, three is even better than two.

The last observation on companionship is about the transfer of power from an elder to a youth. The point is made that a wise youth will gain popularity over a foolish elder. However, Solomon implies that the young wise youth may grow to be old and foolish when he says, "Yet those who come afterward will not rejoice with him." We can use Solomon as an example in that as he got older, he became more foolish. I don't think it is to be concluded that rulers always grow foolish with age, but it certainly is a likelihood given this verse. Solomon says this is vanity and grasping for the wind because this cycle will repeat like the cycles he mentioned in chapter 1.

Chapter 5

First Commands
5:1-8

Solomon now shifts to direct commands to the reader. This section is much more akin to the first nine chapters of Proverbs.

5:1

The first command is to walk prudently when you go to worship, speaking contextually of walking to the temple Solomon built. We are the Church and do not go the house of God that Solomon was referencing, but we can apply this truth to when we gather together as believers to worship God. "Prudent" is not a word used much anymore, but it means "sensible." We are next instructed to listen carefully instead of paying attention to fools. Solomon indicates that being foolish around a worshipful gathering is evil and fools are unaware of that fact.

5:2-3

The following commands deal with our speech.

From the book of Proverbs we know that Solomon is very aware of the pitfalls of using our speech unwisely, as there are at least sixty-five proverbs that deal directly with the subject of our speech. "Do not be quick with your speech," [sic] Solomon says, especially when talking to God. Why? Because God is in Heaven, and you are not. I believe this is a matter of perspective. Since God knows the heritage He is giving to everyone and can see everything from beginning to end (Acts 15:18), be careful not to speak quickly and then regret it.

The next verse is a parallel proverb. The two subjects are a dream and a fool's words. The modifiers of these subjects are much activity and many words respectively. The connection may be that a dream in which you get many ideas would cause you to do something foolish, which happens because you are participating in too much activity.

5:4-7

Solomon moves on to vows, continuing his emphasis on being careful with speech. He comments it is foolish to make a vow and then delay its action. Why is it better to not vow if you are not going to act? Because it is being untruthful with your words.

Furthermore, neither make promises that end in causing you to sin, nor say your promise was in error before the messenger of God. God is not happy when we cause ourselves to sin through our speech and is even angry when we make excuses for it. The ideas you get from your dreams (which come from too much activity) and many words (a fool's voice) is vanity Solomon says. Then he adds "but fear God." If you had feared and trusted God in the first place, you would not be in the sinning position you are in now. Better to do something right the first time than deal with the consequences of your folly.

5:8

The final command in this section deals with the injustice that Solomon observed back in 3:16. Basically, don't be surprised when there is inequality in a country or city. He next references the chain of command that works within a province. Solomon may be indicating what happens in this chain is what we would call "passing the buck," allowing injustice to happen because no one takes responsibility for it. It could also be a reference to Solomon's proverbs about a ruler becoming wicked because of his surrounding influences or lack of counsel (Proverbs 14:28, 28:2, 29:12). Another possibility is since all men are sinful, sinners rule over sinners and we should expect sinful behavior throughout the chain of command. This sinful behavior can even be amplified because of the power political offices hold. Any of these interpretations could be right or all three. The point of the proverb is to not be surprised at oppression or perverse behavior in a province.

Chapter 7

Money and Possessions
5:9-20

The sections between 5:9 and 8:1 are difficult to outline when looking at the overall structure of Ecclesiastes. Each of the sections (5:9-20, 6:1-12, 7:1-14, 7:15-8:1) have a similar structure to the points Solomon is making, usually with a main theme throughout. Each have references to things he is personally observing, including proverbial statements, and have personal conclusions. It would be plausible to lump all of these sections into one big section when creating a macro outline of this book, but I have decided to split them into separate chapters, as I think the separate conclusions in each segment warrant individual attention.

The proverbs and statements in the rest of chapter 5 all deal with material things.

5:9-11

Verse 9 talks about the profit of the land being for all- that profit being food and other resources. The next proverb is very important when understanding the money and material possessions received in a person's life and the desire for them. If you love having these things, you will never be satisfied by how much you have. Why is this vanity? Because it will not belong to you after you die.

The following proverb speaks to the use of resources. If a man produces more goods, there will be more consumers of those goods. This could be by families growing or more people moving to the area of increase. The only profit the owners or producers of these goods receive is that they see that there is more. They may gain more money from selling them, but as the previous proverb states, they will not be satisfied with this.

"Honest work produces sweet sleep" [sic] the next proverb says whether you have many possessions or few. Even if you have many things, they will not give you rest. Only restful sleep from a hard day of labor will refresh you. The implication here may be that the rich don't work hard, given that the word "but" is used as a word of contrast.

5:12-17

Solomon now talks about two severe evils he has observed. The first is money kept to the hurt of the owner and these riches are gone through misfortune. "Misfortune" is translated by two Hebrew words: work and evil. Where this misfortune or evil work comes from is not stated. It could come from the person or from sources outside that person's control.

The rest of verse 14 is almost repeated in verse 16 as a severe evil. Verse 15 states that we brought nothing into this world, and we will bring nothing out, while 16 asks the question "what profit has he who has labored for the wind?" The implied answer is nothing. Two comments are then added in verse 17: the owner of the lost riches eats in darkness all his days, and he has much sorrow, sickness, and anger. What a shame to work so hard for riches and to later realize their worthless value. May we spend our time on work that has eternal value instead of laboring for the wind.

5:18-20

Verse 18 is our next of 6 conclusions but is missing an element we have seen in the previous three. "Nothing is better" is missing and the phrase, "it is good and fitting" replaces it. The word translated "fitting" in Hebrew means "proper" or "pertaining to what corresponds to an expectation." Solomon may be building on the fact that it is our heritage and expectation to enjoy our work, as he mentions it being our heritage at the end of this verse.

The next two verses seem to be gentle counsel to those with possessions that the origin of their wealth is God. He has given them wealth, riches, and power to enjoy those things. They have received that heritage from Him and the ability to rejoice in their labor. All of these are gifts from God.

There are two Hebrew words that translate "dwell unduly" in verse 20. I believe a better translation comes out of the King James which translates the Hebrew "not much remember," as the two words mean "to increase" and "to remember" respectfully. The verse means that the rich man to whom God has given the aforementioned gifts would not much remember his past days, because there is so much joy in his life. The Hebrew word translated "keeps him busy" is the word for "afflicted." God "afflicts" this man with the joy of his heart. God is the source of any wealth we may possess. God wants us to enjoy it! He also gives us guidance on how to use it. Do not feel guilty for wealth; enjoy it and use it wisely, understanding from Whom it was given.

Chapter 8

Labor
6:1-12

After explaining where wealth originates and what to think about it in the previous chapter, Solomon begins chapter 6 with an evil that he has seen often in his days.

6:1-2

The person he describes is very similar to the man in 5:18-20, yet he is not given the ability to enjoy his possessions. They are instead consumed by a foreigner. This situation is mentioned as being a great affliction. Psychologically, it is devastating to see the work of your hands go into the hands of another.

6:3-6

The next group of verses is comparing a man who is not satisfied with goodness or a proper burial (likely meaning no one close enough to him to give a burial) to a stillborn child. We have already seen that Solomon praised those who have never existed above those who must toil on the Earth (4:3). The natural tendency, as it was in 4:3, is to start interpreting these verses with eternal truths revealed later in Scripture, thus making this section hard to understand. If we only consider the temporal nature of our lives, as is Solomon's intent, it is better for a stillborn child than us. This child comes in vanity, which is what our work is worth, and leaves in darkness, which is what happens to us when we die. What the child is missing is all the toil in between those two events. In this context of temporal affliction on Earth and not factoring in eternal blessing in Heaven, Solomon's conclusion is accurate.

6:7-9

Verse 7 tells us no matter how much of our labor we consume, our soul is never satisfied. If a wise man has more than a fool, neither one is satisfied with their work. Solomon next asks, "does the poor man who knows proper social etiquette have anything that will satisfy his soul?" No. It is better to be content with what you possess than looking for what you do not have to satisfy your soul. In the end, all labor for our mouth is vanity and grasping for the wind anyway.

6:10-12

The following three verses deal with our identity

as humans. We are mankind, and we will be nothing more, nothing less. God will be God, and there is nothing we can do about it. Solomon now asks three questions: Does man have an advantage over any other being since his life is lived in vanity? Does anyone know what is good for a man? Does man know the future, especially what will happen after he dies? The answers to these questions all lie with God.

There is no advantage to being a man, but God gives him grace, which is greater than anything else a man may receive. No one knows what is good for man, except God. No man can know the future, but God knows the future. Whenever we ask any questions about the labor in which we toil, God has all the answers we need. How do we get these answers from Him? By praying and studying His written word to us.

Chapter 9

Comparisons and Wisdom
7:1-14

In this section Solomon gives us a number of "better than" comparisons in the first ten verses. He then sums up these observations by talking about some wisdom principles and how we should see life as it is happening.

7:1-4

The first four verses all deal with the subject mourning and death. The first proverb states that a good name/reputation is better precious ointment. I believe we are to gather from this proverb that it is better to have a good standing among men than material things that take care of your appearance.

The next proverb hearkens back to 4:3 and 6:1-6, talking about the positive aspects of death. From Solomon's perspective of only factoring in temporal life and its profit, our day of death would be better than our birth. The latter is ending our toil, while the former is beginning it. With the revelation of the New Testament, we know that when we die, a believer will go straight to the presence of the Lord (2 Corinthians

5:6-8, Philippians 1:22-23). We could argue on these grounds that the day we die is better than our birth. But Solomon is not considering that fact; he is only talking about temporal toil and life on Earth. This theme will pop up again in chapter 9 of Ecclesiastes, where we will discuss another aspect of how Solomon is viewing earthly life.

Proverb number three tells us to go to the house of mourning after a death so we will be faced with our own mortality. Verse 9 continues this thought, telling us our heart is made better by sorrow rather than laughter. The last verse on this thought contrasts the wise being where mourning is occurring as opposed to a fool being were mirth/joy is occurring.

This is a bit odd to hear after we have been told twice to rejoice in all our labor (3:12, 2:22). However, we have also been told that mirth does not accomplish anything (2:1-2). Putting all this together, I suggest that a wise man cannot fully rejoice in his labor without understanding the sorrow that comes from looking at the vanity of our earthly life. If we don't spend time contemplating the sorrow and vanity of our accomplishments and life (as Solomon will call our life vain later) we cannot rejoice in our labor because we may still be holding on to the idea that something we do is going to last. To apply this truth from Ecclesiastes, Jesus best sums it up:

> Do not lay up for yourselves treasures on earth, where moth and rust destroy and where thieves

break in and steal; but lay up for yourselves treasures in heaven, where neither moth nor rust destroys and where thieves do not break in and steal.
Matthew 6:19-20

7:5-6

The next proverb gives us a comparison and then a simile to help us understand it better. Hearing the rebuke of the wise so we have the opportunity to learn from it is better than the song of fools, which doesn't have any content in order to gain knowledge. It is interesting that Solomon uses thorns to describe a fool's laughter in the next verse, because thorns are not useful for anything when they are alive. When you burn them after the plant dies, you may get a short burst of fame, but they become nothing but ash after that, which is thrown out. The laughter of the fool is the same way. Fools are foolish, so there is nothing to be gained from them in the first place. When they laugh, you might laugh too, getting some enjoyment from what is said, but after the laugh is over, there is nothing left to be used. What vanity, as Solomon comments.

7:7

Verse 7 has two points about evil destroying a man's mindset. When a wise man is oppressed, it can do many things to his psyche. He may not keep God's precepts (Psalm 119:134), he will be diminished and brought low (Psalm 107:39), it brings trouble upon him (Psalm 55:3), and ultimately destroys his ability to think, as our current verse says. A bribe also debases or destroys the mind of a man, here symbolized by the word heart.

7:8-10

The Hebrew word translated "thing" in verse 8 means "a happening" in this context, but it often deals with speech or statements. The other meaning would work well here too, as the lasting effects of a statement are better than the initial response. Easily understood is the next proverb as well: the patient or slow to anger attitude is better than the proud attitude. Verse 9 continues this idea, adding that anger rests in the bosom or heart of fools.

The next verse could be taken by itself, but I believe it is also continuing the idea of being patient or slow to anger. Implied in the question "why were the former days better than these" is a hint of resentment for why the current days are not enjoyable. This resentment could even be or lead into anger. Not only is anger not good as the previous proverb states, but according to 6:16, we don't know what is good for us or what will happen in the future. It could be that the goodness of the former days allowed you to relax too much, which has led to your current situation. Or the badness of the current days allows God to shape you into the person He wants you to be. We should take each moment as it comes with the right attitude, which is to enjoy our heritage given by God and trust him throughout our heritage.

7:11-12

According to verse 11, an inheritance is good when you use it wisely (Proverbs 13:22, 20:21). "Those who see the sun" just means those who are alive. An inheritance to the dead will do nothing. Why is it good to use an inheritance wisely? Because that wealth may give you a defense when you need it, but better than money is having wisdom when facing a trial requiring a defense.

7:13-14

Verses 13 and 14 sound like a conclusion, but do not follow the same pattern of conclusions as the rest of the book. I believe it is best to approach these verses as a conclusion, as the next verse is returning to Solomon's observations which we have not seen since 6:1. It is also a more general statement about temporal life, unlike the first twelve verses of chapter 7.

That said, when we observe God's works, we cannot change anything that He has set in motion. We have already seen this principle in 3:14-15.

The next verse is such a powerful truth, connected directly to verse 10. When things are going well, rejoice! When things are not going well, meditate on the fact that God gives you both good and bad as your heritage. Why does He do this? So that man learns to trust Him. Since we don't know what is good for us (6:12) and we should not look back longingly to "the good ol' days" (7:10), should we not look to the One who gives us these happenings and trust that He has our best interests at heart?

Chapter 10

More Observations and a Conclusion
7:15 - 8:1

We return to Solomon's personal observations, centering around righteousness and wisdom, and two conclusions about wisdom and women.

7:15

Verse 15 deals with an inequality in life from our perspective: sometimes righteous people die young and wicked people live longer. Solomon approached this subject earlier in 3:16-17, comforting us that God will take care of this through His righteousness. Notice that neither spot says it is an evil or it is vanity. From our perspective, it is hard for us to see how God is going to rectify this disparity. But if God appoints days of prosperity and adversity (7:13-14), then it is better to trust Him rather than figuring out when justice will be done.

7:16-17

In my opinion, the next two verses are two of the most difficult verses in the Bible to understand. The consistent message of scripture is to become more righteous, or sanctified, constantly. But here we are told not to be overly righteous nor overly wise. The reason given by Solomon is that we will destroy ourselves if we do so. The word translated "overly" means "to increase or become more numerous." I believe what is being said is the pursuit of gaining more righteousness and wisdom can ultimately be your demise, as you try in vain to figure out every little detail or the reason for everything.

Deuteronomy says:

> The secret things belong to the LORD our God, but those things which are revealed belong to us and to our children forever, that we may do all the words of this law.
> *Deuteronomy 29:29*

Notice that there are things which God has not revealed to us but what He has revealed we can understand and apply.

The New Testament echoes this fact in Romans:

> Oh, the depth of the riches both of the wisdom and knowledge of God! How unsearchable are His judgements and His ways past finding out!
> *Romans 11:33*

Considering verse 15 of Ecclesiastes talks about an inequality we will not understand while on this

Earth, I believe the correct way to interpret verse 16 is that the pursuit of being overly righteous or wise leads to destruction because there are things we simply cannot know.

A later-revealed truth in Colossians may also help us understand this verse:

> Therefore, if you died with Christ from the basic principles of the world, why, as though living in the world, do you subject yourselves to regulations- "do not touch, do not taste, do not handle," which all concern things which perish with the using – according to the commandments and doctrines of men? These things indeed have an appearance of wisdom in self-imposed religion, false humility, and neglect of the body, but are of no value against the indulgence of the flesh.
> *Colossians 2:20-23*

If you try to increase your righteousness through man-made commandments, you may start to think you are in some way responsible for you sanctification or salvation, which you are not (Ephesians 2:8-9, Romans 8:11). That mindset will destroy a believer because they cannot live an effective life for God when they increase in self-made righteousness.

Verse 17 is a caution to not go too far to the other end of the spectrum by being overly wicked or foolish. In the same way that Romans 6:1 warns us to not sin even though more sin produces more grace, this verse warns us to not be foolish even though more righteousness and wisdom leads to destruction.

I don't think by Solomon saying "do not be overly foolish" he is prescribing to be a little foolish. Foolishness in Solomon's writings is always bad. Instead, Solomon is cautioning that too much foolishness and wickedness will lead to an early death, a concept echoed in James 1:15.

Verse 18 gives us the reason we should grasp these concepts and apply them: he who fears or trusts in God will escape destruction from too much wisdom and death from too much foolishness.

7:19-20

Verse 19 explains that wisdom strengthens the wise more than ten rulers of a city. This is telling us it is better to seek God's wisdom to be self-sufficient than depend on other authorities to make you stronger. Why is that the case? Because there is not a just man on Earth who does not sin. The wisdom of God is pure and will keep you on the straight path more than if you were to depend on others' so-called wisdom, which is corrupted by sin just as you are.

7:21-22

Solomon says do not take to heart every statement

that is made, lest you hear your servant curse you. We will all be slandered behind our back eventually. Do not go looking for what others think of you, or you will hear it. We should know this because we have done the same thing, Solomon adds.

7:23-25

The Preacher begins a conclusion at verse 23 that is different from the other conclusions in Ecclesiastes. By "all," I believe Solomon is talking about all the proverbs, starting from chapter 6 until now. He says "I will be wise" alluding to the pride that comes from believing you have everything figured out. But the reality is that knowing everything proved to be far from Solomon. He found out that the more he learned, the more he didn't know. In fact, his next statement about wisdom being exceedingly deep, he asks the question "who can find it out?" "Exceedingly deep" is translated by the repetition of the same Hebrew word that means "deep" and implies what is difficult or even impossible to know (Proverbs 18:4). The implied answer is no one; no one can find out the wisdom that God has not revealed.

Solomon's pursuit is restated in 7:25, but he adds "the reason of things" here. Solomon originally set out to just understand all the things done under heaven in 1:13 and 1:17. However, as soon as he started seeing the vanity of it all, I believe he started asking questions about the reason things are the way they are. That is why we get the statements in 1:15 and 1:18 right after he explains what he's doing. Solomon learns through this pursuit that there are some things that just happen and we can't always know or understand the reason they happen.

7:26-29

In verse 26 through 29 Solomon starts telling us about good and bad women. This must have been on his mind after talking about things he couldn't figure out (am I right, men?). Even though it might seem odd to put this subject right after 7:23-25, I think Solomon is sharing observations he discovered through his pursuit (1:13, 1:17). This does fit Solomon's overall structure of observations about life mixed in with proverbial sections.

Solomon had trouble with women (1 Kings 11:1) and this section may be admitting his mistake that ultimately led to the kingdom on Israel being torn in half (1 Kings 11:11-13). Solomon would know getting wrapped up with a woman whose heart is snares and nets is more bitter than death. He says the sinner will be trapped by her and Solomon was. A man who pleases or does good for God will not be trapped by her. The consequences for Solomon's sin were grave. We should be wise to not make the same mistake.

Solomon next refers to himself as the Preacher for the first time since 1:12. I believe this is because he is sharing his wisdom with a younger generation to help them avoid the errors he made. Solomon sums up what he has learned by saying "adding one thing to the other to find out the reason" (7:27) but he also admits that he hasn't found reasons for everything in verse 28. Solomon poetically says in the next verse that he rarely has found good men or women even when looking at a thousand people.

In Proverbs 31:10, the writer says that a virtuous woman is worth far above rubies. There are multiple mentions of wisdom and knowledge being more precious than rubies throughout Proverbs, but only a virtuous wife is mentioned as being far above them. Solomon is saying that wisdom is the most precious thing to get (Proverbs 4:7), and the next best thing is a good wife. Men, let's learn this lesson well and realize how great a gift our wives are!

> Houses and riches are an inheritance from fathers
> But a prudent wife is from the LORD.
> *Proverbs 19:14*

7:29-8:1

Moving away from the subject of women, Solomon gives us something we can know on the heels of admitting he cannot know everything.

God making man upright is a reference to the creation of man in the Garden of Eden, because we know we are conceived in sin (Psalm 51:5). But it was our choice to seek out schemes. This verse alone proves that we have free will and God does not force us to do anything. It is also a good reminder that God originally made us perfect, but it is our fault that the world is in the state we currently experience. What an encouragement to put your faith in God and look forward to the day in which things will be made perfect again!

Armed with these truths about women and ourselves, Solomon asks questions about who is wise and who can interpret a thing, probably a reference back to the reason of things in chapter 7. Wisdom is the answer. It makes our face shine so that others may see wisdom in us and learn from it. It also gives our face sternness; the Hebrew word translated here means "a condition in which one can exert great force or withstand great force." We are able to fight and defend ourselves with wisdom, as well as draw others to us. No wonder Proverbs tells us to pursue wisdom above all else (Proverbs 4:7).

Chapter 11

The King and Us
8:2-9

In this short section there are a few commands and observations about how subjects are to act toward the king. Even if there is not a king in the nation we live, this is still very practical advice for how to treat those in power.

8:2-9

Solomon's first command is to keep the king's commands, which is the same idea echoed in Romans 13:1-7. We are to act this way because law abiding citizens will have a better testimony than law breakers. Of course, this is assuming the commands you obey do not break God's commands. In this case, we are to follow God, as Peter and John did before their rulers, elders, and scribes (Acts 4:19-20).

We are also not to leave his presence quickly, meaning that you are to let the king finish with you rather than you finishing with him. Solomon next describes the tension between obeying the king and obeying God. When it says, "he does whatever pleases him," Solomon is inferring that kings act how they want without regard to the law. Often times think they are above the law (Deuteronomy 17:20). If this is the case, then we must be careful to not follow the king too closely or else we may find ourselves defending an evil thing.

Verse 4 tells us that the authority of the king is absolute in his domain, and no one may challenge it. Whenever we follow his authority, we are not harmed. Solomon then issues a warning: we are to discern the time and judgement of the commands placed on us. Why? Because for every matter there is a time and judgement (3:1-8, 3:16-17). However, there is increasing misery of a man through these times. Not only can the misery occur directly because of a king's command but through the grief of bad decisions and knowing there are consequences down the road. But we do not know exactly what these consequences will be as verse 7 says. If we do not know what will happen, we don't know when things will happen either. Better to trust God than to depend on a king/ruler to make life better.

The word translated "spirit" in verse 8 is the same word for "wind." I believe it could be translated either way here. If it is translated "spirit," then verse 8 is a parallel proverb saying that we cannot retain our spirit when we die or have power in the moment of death. If the word is translated "wind," it is a proverb stating that we cannot control our circumstances and we cannot overcome death. Given that the previous statement is about our inability to know what and when something will happen in reference to dealing with a king's commands, I prefer "wind" as the translation. Either way, there is "no release from that war" of catching the wind or avoiding death. The last statement of verse 9 can fit with wind or spirit because wicked people generally try to control their circumstances and deliver themselves from death, which they do not have power over.

Here is how I would sum up verse 9: We cannot control our circumstances, nor when we will die. If you follow a wicked path, you may try to win this war of uncertainty by controlling your circumstances and thinking you can have power over your time of death. But you will not be delivered from this war: you will always fight against the unknown.

In the verse that follows Solomon is observing the evil that rulers often hurt themselves when ruling over others. This may be a reference to Solomon knowing there was discontentment in his kingdom (1 Kings 11:26). This hurt caused Jeroboam and the people to rebel against Rehoboam and tore apart the kingdom. Whenever we come into positions of authority, we must heed this verse carefully.

Chapter 12

The Reality of Death
8:10 - 9:10

This is the last section in which we get a very personal look into Solomon's thoughts. We get two conclusions in this segment, which are both very powerful. The rest of the book is devoted to Solomon passing on his wisdom to subsequent generations.

8:10-13

Solomon sees the dead in a processional being carried outside the city and buried. They are soon forgotten. Solomon comments that this is vanity, just like the vanity he observed in chapter 6. He then looks at the living and sees that sons of men are doing evil because they are not punished quickly after their evil acts. Solomon then rests on the principle that things generally go well for those who fear God. Conversely, it is also true that things generally will not be well for those who do not fear God. They may live a long time while doing evil, but even a long life is but a shadow, and he will be judged for his works (3:17).

8:14-9:2

Solomon next tells of a vanity wherein bad things happen to good people and good things happen to bad people. Vanity is used to introduce the statement and the situation is called vanity. The double use of the word emphasizes what a vanity this is.

What is described in verse 14 is one of the major aspects of what we typically call the "problem of evil." The problem is typically stated as "if there is an all-good god, why is there evil in the world?" This question is debated at the high philosophical level, but most people deal with this problem in the sense of what Solomon just described- that bad things happen to good people and vice-versa. Typically, I hear Christians develop very beautiful and well-constructed philosophical answers to this question. I am not going to say that it is bad to answer the question in this way, but it is always striking how the Bible answers questions such as these in such a simple manner.

Ecclesiastes' answer to why bad things happen to good people and vice-versa is vanity. Or, to state it in a modern conversational way, "You're going to die, so why does it matter?" A bit unsettling, but Solomon goes further by telling you what you should do about it in our final (and my favorite) "nothing is better" statement. He commends enjoyment and says "Eat, drink, and be merry!" Why? Because that will be with you during your labor in your days that God gives you on Earth. Nothing else will last from your work, but these three things will always be present when you appreciate Who the toil is from.

The next three verses give us what I think is the most personal conclusion found in Ecclesiastes. Verse 16 restates Solomon's pursuit from chapter 2. What is the ultimate conclusion? When you pursue understanding, you will see all the work of God and not be able to find out the reason for it. If a man works to discover it, you will not find it. If a wise man uses his wisdom to try to discover it, he will not find the reason for it.

After considering all that he has learned throughout this pursuit, Solomon tells us his conclusion: all the work of the righteous and wise are in the hand or power of God. Do we know all the reasons for why we have this work? We know the reasons that have been revealed in God's Word (1:13, 3:10, and 3:18), but can we know the whole of everything and the reasons for each thing? No. Better to realize and apply Solomon's conclusions than live your whole life incorrectly and come to the same conclusion much later on your own.

9:2-6

Solomon continues his look into death by commenting that people don't know love or hatred by what they see. Why? Because we don't know what is good or bad for us (6:12). He says all things come

8:10 - 9:10

alike, meaning that we all receive similar work while here on Earth. He then contrasts different kinds of people through the rest of verse 2. The one evil thing that happens to us all in verse 3 is death. Why is death evil? Because it was the consequence of disobeying God (Genesis 2:16-17). There was no death before the Fall, therefore it must be evil.

Solomon says our hearts are full of evil, a great verse to keep in mind if someone says that people are basically good. The word translated "madness" means "an extreme lack of understanding and wisdom." We are evil while we're on earth, and then we die. But we have hope while we live, because we can trust God and His commandments which can make us more sanctified. Solomon uses the analogy that a living dog has more hope than a dead lion, precisely because the dog is alive.

As we come to verse 5, it is worth restating that the context of Ecclesiastes is only talking about temporal things, not eternal or afterlife truths. When Solomon says that the dead know nothing, he is not saying that there is no afterlife or that the dead are in some sort of soul sleep. He is saying that all the temporal things we know while living are not known by the dead simply because they are no longer living. There is no temporal reward because they are no longer on Earth. They are forgotten, because eventually all those that remember them also die. Their love, hatred and envy also no longer exist because they are not on earth to have those emotions.

The last statement in verse 6 tells us we are correct in interpreting these verses this way: it says they don't share or experience anything under the sun.

9:7-10

What should we do with all this truth? Enjoy our bread and drink wine happily. Why? Because God has accepted or delighted in your works. Live life to the fullest with white garments and lacking no oil on your head, which is a mark of respect. Live joyfully with your wife during your life that God has given you. But during all this encouragement, we are hit with a reality: our life is vanity.

In verse 9 Solomon calls our life vain and our days vanity. This seems discouraging, but it isn't given the context of Ecclesiastes. Nothing you do in this life will last, making your earthly life all vanity. However, whatever you find to do, do with all you might because God expects that of us. He has given us all the labor in which we toil; to not work with all our ability would be to waste what God has given us.

The second half of verse 10 is stating that when you die the portion God gave you while on this Earth will be over. It is not saying that we do not think and therefore cease to exist, as the Jehovah's Witnesses interpret this verse. It is a conclusion saying in the modern vernacular "you only have one life to live." Nothing done in your portion will last, so use it wisely and enjoy it for God has given it to you!

Chapter 13

The Return
9:11 - 10:20

After the uplifting conclusion at 9:10, Solomon returns from his pursuit to teach us a number of proverbs and life lessons that take us almost to the end of the book. It could be argued that 11:9-12:8 has a very similar feel to this section and is one continuous thought, but I have separated these into two parts because the last section has more of a direct charge to the reader, specifically a young man, whereas this segment is more general.

9:11-12

Solomon observes that no matter how swift, strong, wise, understanding, or skilled a man is, the passing of time and chance happen to everyone. A man's positive attributes will not always yield success, because chance can change an outcome no matter the effort or planning that went into an action. This does not mean we don't try hard, don't plan, or don't care about the outcome of a thing, but simply that we have to deal with chance happenings.

Because of chance, we don't know when evil

times are going to come upon us as fish and birds don't know when they are going to be caught. However, there is no chance from God's perspective. Known to God are all His works from the beginning (Acts 15:18) and that includes the heritage that He gives us (3:22). Furthermore, studying the Hebrew word translated "chance" gives us more insight into this concept. The definition is "an event that happens, implying that it may be a random occurrence, or have an appearance of chance." It may appear to us as chance because we do not know the future, but we can trust that it is not chance to God and He always has everything under control. Has it ever dawned on you that nothing dawns on God?

9:13-18

Solomon next gives us a short story with a lesson that he learned from the following situation: a great king set up a siege at a small city and the city was delivered by the wisdom of a poor man, but no one remembered him. We learn that wisdom is better than strength, as seen by the illustration of a small city with few defenses being able to stand against great might using wisdom. Nevertheless, Solomon says, a poor man is not listened to and his wisdom is hated.

Quiet, wise words should be listened to rather than loud, foolish ones, verse 17 states. We should remember this verse during discussions in which we find ourselves or others talking over each other.

Verse 18 adds that wisdom is better than weapons, however one sinner can destroy the good gained by wisdom. May we apply wisdom over force in our battles and not destroy good with sin.

10:1

In the same way dead flies ruin perfume, so does a little folly ruin a person who is known for wisdom. How often we see how one mistake a respected man makes can ruin his reputation and everything he has worked for.

10:2

This verse contrasts the right and left hand with wisdom and folly, respectively. In the Hebrew culture, the right hand was considered more useful than the left. We can also see the emphasis on the right hand being in a position of power throughout the Old Testament (ex. Isaiah 41:10). This proverb is stating that our heart is to be in the more useful position if we are to be wise.

10:3

Wherever a fool goes he is foolish and shows everyone he is a fool.

10:4

If a ruler gets angry with you, do not panic and leave your post or office. The Hebrew word translated "conciliation" can mean "calmness" or "gentleness." If you flee, you cannot explain yourself or seek reconciliation. If you are calm, it can pacify great offenses.

10:5-7

Solomon observes another evil in verse 5, and it is an error in judgement from a ruler. The ruler upholds folly, while the rich, assumed here to be not foolish, are not given dignity. Princes are not in their proper position on a horse, but instead servants are in their place. Solomon is talking about the proper order of things, that folly should not have dignity and the rich and princes should be in their proper place.

It is easy for us to look at Jesus, the ultimate Ruler, and see a contradiction between His humbleness and Solomon's comments. I don't think we are to read that into these verses. I believe Solomon is simply saying that there is an order to hierarchy, and it should be followed. The rich and princes should be held in respect for their positions because that is orderly. The point is that folly should not be exalted, which can be seen when the government hierarchy is out of order. Those in positions of power should be humble, but we should also respect them for the office they hold.

10:8-10

Next, we are given four examples of how we can be hurt by the work in which we engage and a lesson in light of this. If you are cutting down a tree and your axe head is dull, you can still cut down the tree, but it will take more strength. It would be wiser to sharpen the edge to make the job easier and faster. Instead of "wisdom brings success" in the conclusion of verse 10, a more literal translation is, "the advantage of wisdom brings success." Even though you can get a job done because of strength, that does not mean you should be unwise about how you go about performing a task. As we would say in the modern vernacular, "work smarter, not harder."

10:11-14

Solomon spends the next four verses dealing with a fool's speech. As a serpent may bite when it is not charmed, so a man who talks a lot is no different. The Hebrew word translated "babbler" is the same word for "tongue." We can gather from this that if a tongue is not entertained (Proverbs 18:8), it may hurt someone. In a similar way, the words of the fool will consume him while the words of the wise gain or give favor.

When listening to a fool, Solomon gives us five things to look out for: the first thing a fool says is foolish, the last thing said is also foolish, he uses a lot of words, no one knows what he is going to say next, and you can't tell him what will happen to him because you don't know what he said in the first place! We should be on guard against these things both when we are listening and speaking.

10:15

A fool is so wearied by simple tasks that he doesn't even know how to go to the city to do what he needs to do!

10:16-17

A woe is set upon a land whose king is a child. Because foolishness is bound up in the heart of a child (Proverbs 22:15), a child ruler cannot be wise. Why? Because as the ruler, the rod of discipline will not be applied to him which would remove his foolishness. Princes feasting in the morning is probably a reference to government officials not doing their jobs but instead taking advantage of their position and incorrectly using the people's resources. In contrast, a blessing is placed on a land when the ruler is the son of nobles. Although we often see generational nobility not ruling well, the idea in this verse is that a ruler's son would have been trained by his father to govern well. In this blessed land, the princes feast at the proper time, showing respect for the office the hold. They also hold the feast for the correct reason: not to party for the sake of having a good time and getting drunk but celebrating strength.

10:18

All things decay over time, especially a dwelling place. But if you are not lazy, you will refresh the house and it will not decay to an unlivable state nor will the roof leak.

10:19

When you have a feast, have a good time with wine, causing some of the merriness. But money will always get things done. Solomon would know this to be very true (2 Chronicles 1:15). Feasting should be used properly to celebrate, but money can always be used instead.

10:20

Do not curse the king or the rich, as someone may hear you and tell someone else your thoughts. This verse also may be where the phrase "a little bird told me" came from, even though that exact phrase doesn't appear here. Even if that isn't the case, it is wise to not reveal any bad thoughts about those in authority, lest they find out about it.

Chapter 14

Observations About Work
11:1-8

In this section, Solomon gives us four observations about how to conduct our work during our earthly life. Even though all our days are vanity, that doesn't mean we squander the heritage God has given us. When we apply these principles to our work, we will be prepared when chance happens to our plans.

11:1

Casting bread upon the waters is telling us to prepare for evil times. We can store food away and find it later when evil times come to us.

11:2

Giving servings to eight tells us to be generous with our resources because we do not know who will help us in the time of trouble. Make friends with your resources and they will be there for you when you need them (see also Luke 16:9).

11:1-8

11:3-4

Do not pay too much attention to the weather or anticipate what may happen in nature. If you do this, you will not start you work, nor will you finish it. We should prepare for circumstances beyond our control, but they should not paralyze us from working to take care of ourselves.

11:5-6

Solomon next restates the fact that we do not know the reason God does things, just as we do not know how the wind will behave or how a child will grow in their mother's womb. That being the case, we should work in the morning and not stop working at night. We don't know which of these acts will help us in the future so we should not "put all our eggs in one basket." Diversifying our work or investments is a good strategy because some things will fail and others succeed.

11:7-8

Verse 7 tells us to enjoy the light and sun in our lives. But Solomon quickly reminds us to also remember the bad days, and that there is no profit to our work. This proverb is bringing together all the conclusions about enjoying our heritage but balancing that with his observation that wisdom is found in the tough parts of life (7:1-4). Keep these things in their proper perspective and you will succeed in enjoying life in the correct way because all that is coming is vanity.

Chapter 15

To the Young Man
11:9 - 12:8

In a very personal way, Solomon now directly addresses any young person- specifically here a man- that is reading Ecclesiastes.

11:9-12:1

He tells this man to rejoice because he is young; walk in the ways he sees fit given what he sees with his eyes, assuming that the young person is following after God. Because of these things, a young person should remove sorrow from their heart and not do evil because the foolishness of youth is vanity.

The Preacher tells the youth to remember God as the Creator, to build a foundation that will stand when difficult days come and before old age causes a man to have no pleasure in his days.

12:2-5

The next four verses bring up many things that happen in life, which all have the central point that your body deteriorates as you get older, but the world remains. Your keepers or hands begin to tremble, you will not stand up as straight, your grinders or teeth fall out, and your eyes do not see as well as they used to. Your hearing gets worse and you wake up early from small sounds like a bird but you can't hear loud things like music as well. Heights now scare you as well as things in your way, insects become burdens, and motivation fails. All these things happen in old age and then you die.

12:6-8

Verse 6 and 7 talks about things that happen in death, as well as the reality that we are but dust and our spirit will return to our Creator.

I believe 12:1-7 are a way of saying "enjoy life while you have it." What a simple message after the great detail and advice that Solomon has shared throughout the book! Solomon then concludes in verse 8 his pursuit that he started in chapter 2 by ending the way he began in 1:2: "Vanity of vanities" says the Preacher, "All is vanity."

We have ended where we began in assessing temporal life but with much more understanding of how to conduct ourselves and think about our days throughout life. There is yet an afterword by Solomon, but the pursuit of understanding all that is done under the sun has been closed.

Chapter 16

Solomon's Afterword
12:9-14

Solomon switches to talking about himself in the third person through verse 11, then makes a personal plea to his son and concludes his writing.

12:9-11

Referring to himself as the Preacher, Solomon still taught the people knowledge in his old age. He also never stopped learning, thinking about, and seeking more proverbs. He made sure in his speaking and writing that what he was communicating was the truth. He tells us about truth, saying wise words are like goads or a cattle prod and a well driven nail.

Here is the imagery Solomon is getting at: a nail was often used at the end of a cattle prod to poke animals who did not want to move. Hearing words of wisdom is like being prodded by a sharp nail to get us to move in the correct direction when we are stubborn. How painful it is to be taught to move in this way, but how often it is the only way we learn!

12:12

Solomon then directly addresses his son imploring him to listen to words of wisdom. Books will always be made trying to explain everything in life. While these books can bring clarity in certain areas, we should always regard the Bible as the book above all others when seeking truth. Hopefully this commentary has given a solid foundation in understanding Ecclesiastes, but it should only serve to help you to learn more by personally studying Solomon's final inspired writing. Much studying is wearisome to the flesh, making us aware of what studying may do to our energy.

12:13-14

And now comes the conclusion of the whole matter: fear/trust God and obey Him for this is man's all. Why? Because God will bring all our works to judgement and we will be accountable to them. I pray that through studying Ecclesiastes you trust and obey God. First trust in Jesus is the only one capable of paying your sin debt. By simply trusting in His death and resurrection for your sins, you are given eternal life, which can never be taken away. After your salvation is sealed and your entrance into Heaven secured by your faith in Jesus Christ, obey God, heaping up works that will yield rewards when you get to your final resting place.

12:9-14

But while you are still on Earth, eat, drink, and be merry for that is your heritage!

About the Author

Lucas is a bondservant of Jesus Christ.

www.ingramcontent.com/pod-product-compliance
Lightning Source LLC
Chambersburg PA
CBHW020037120526
44589CB00032B/585